The US Constitution

A Junior Novelization Not Just For Kids

By
STEPHEN GNOZA

ACKNOWLEDGEMENTS

This book is dedicated to all Americans who abide by the rule of law, both when following the laws and when creating new ones.

A special thanks to my loving Mother, my Dad for a solid political upbringing, my cousin David, all my family and Stephanie, for all the support and advice.

"...We hold these truths to be self-evident, that all men are created equal, that they are endowed by their Creator with certain unalienable rights, that among these are life, liberty and the pursuit of happiness. That to secure these rights, governments are instituted among men, deriving their just powers from the consent of the governed. That whenever any form of government becomes destructive to these ends, it is the right of the people to alter or to abolish it, and to institute new government, laying its foundation on such principles and organizing its powers in such form, as to them shall seem most likely to effect their safety and happiness. Prudence, indeed, will dictate that governments long established should not be changed for light and transient causes; and accordingly all experience hath shown that mankind are more disposed to suffer, while evils are sufferable, than to right themselves by abolishing the forms to which they are accustomed. But when a long train of abuses and usurpations, pursuing invariably the same object evinces a design to reduce them under absolute despotism, it is their right, it is their duty, to throw off such government, and to provide new guards for their future security...."

An excerpt from the Declaration of Independence,

By Thomas Jefferson

Table of Contents

Introduction

When I was a kid, I had rules. I had to be in bed at a certain time. I could only play video games for two hours every day. I had to do my homework every night and I had to go to school.

When I was a teenager, I could only take the car when my parents gave me permission. I had to be home by a certain time, or at least give my mom a call and let her know I was okay.

You probably expect me to make a comparison between my parents' rules and our government's laws. You're wrong.

Here is the most important thing you need to know about the Constitution: *The Constitution does not tell you and me what we can or cannot do. The Constitution tells the government what it can and cannot do.*

Your parents yell at you when you misbehave. You may not like it. You may think you know better than your parents. But trust me, they yell at you when you break the rules because the rules are there for a reason.

In many ways, the government is our child. It is the child of the American People. And we, as parents, have set some rules for the government. The Constitution is this set of rules.

Americans need to yell at the government when it misbehaves. When the government does something that is against the rules, such as funding a program it shouldn't be funding or restricting your freedoms, it must be reminded that it has rules to follow.

In this book, we will explore how you can check if the rules are being followed and when it is time for you to yell.

<u>You Are the Boss of the Politicians</u>

If you want to earn some money, you may apply for a job. You could get a job in the mall, a gas station or a pizzeria. Odds are, you'll have a boss. The boss will tell you what you are supposed to do, how you are supposed to do it, when you're supposed to show up and what time you can go home.

If you don't listen to the boss, you'll probably be fired and you will be replaced with someone who can do the job that the boss wants done.

Guess who gives the politicians their jobs? You do! By voting people into office, we are the bosses of the politicians! The job description is very simple: make necessary laws that the Constitution allows you to make. If you don't like what the politicians do, you must tell them what you want done. You must remind them to do their job correctly.

Remember, the government didn't create people. People created the government. We are the bosses of the government.

How Did We Get a Constitution?

After the American colonists declared independence in 1776, the colonies saw themselves as no longer part of Great Britain. So, the colonies became individual States. Essentially, each was its own country. Each State had its own government, army, and laws. However, they thought that uniting would be a good idea. This would be very helpful in fighting the British. If the States worked together, they could win the Revolutionary War.

In 1777, the States wrote the Articles of Confederation. The Articles of Confederation was a document that grouped the States together as the United States and set up a central government (called the Federal Government) to govern the States. There were few powers given to the Federal Government, however, and as a result, many of the States did whatever they wanted and they didn't get along. For example, under the Articles of Confederation, there was no President, Congress could not regulate taxes or business, each State made its own money, and the States had to approve any law passed by Congress.

Several years after the Revolutionary War ended, the States decided that they needed to redo the document.   In 1787, they wrote the US Constitution.   This time, the Constitution gave more power to the Federal Government, but kept strict limitations on what it could and could not do.

Most States did not want to give up their power and be ruled by the Federal Government. The States had joined this union of States for the benefits of trade and a common defense, not to be bossed around by a central government.

Who Has the Power?

When the colonists were under the rule of Great Britain, they were not happy about the amount of control that the king had over their lives. Most of all, they were angry that they had to pay taxes to a faraway king. So, when it came time to write the Constitution, the writers wanted to limit the power of the Federal Government. If there was one thing that the founders didn't want after the Revolutionary War, it was another big, powerful, central government. They wanted each State to have power.

Each State has the power to make laws for itself, as long as the laws don't break the rules of the Constitution. If the people of Utah make a law, it is only a law in Utah. This law would not exist in Maryland, Iowa, or any other State.

The Federal Government can make laws that are laws in every State, but unlike the States, the Federal Government is only allowed to make laws that the Constitution gives it permission to make. If the Constitution does not specifically give the Federal Government permission to make a law, then it is not allowed to make such a law.

A Summary of the Rules

The Legislative Branch
(the House of Representatives & the Senate)

CAN	CAN NOT
Collect taxes	Arrest someone without charging them with a crime
Borrow money and pay debts	
Regulate business between States	Punish someone without a trial
Make immigration laws	Punish someone today for an illegal act if the act was committed before it was made illegal
Make bankruptcy laws	
Punish people who make fake money	
Create post offices and roads	Tax goods between States
Protect inventors and artists' creations	Treat the States unequally
Create lower courts below the Supreme Court	Take money from the Treasury without passing a law and telling the public what it does with the money
Punish pirates or traitors	Give people titles of nobility
Declare war	Restrict freedom of speech, assembly, and religious practice
Create and raise money for an army and navy	
Call on State militias for help	Prevent people from voting based on race, gender, or age (if 18 or older)
Train militias	
Create a district for the government (Washington DC)	Tax people for the ability to vote
Make any laws necessary to let the government do its job	
Make laws for electing Senators	

The Executive Branch

(the President)

CAN	CAN NOT
Command the armed forces	Make laws
Pardon someone for a crime	Declare war
Appoint ambassadors, ministers, Supreme Court judges	Increase his salary
Propose laws to Congress	
Propose treaties to Congress	

The Judicial Branch

(the Courts)

CAN	CAN NOT
Decide if a law that Congress passes follows the rules of the Constitution	Make laws
Decide if a treaty follows the rules of the Constitution	Require excessive bail
Try somebody for treason	Impose cruel or unusual punishments
Overrule (reverse) the decision of a lower court	Put a person on trial for the same crime twice
Issue a warrant that allows a person's property to be searched or taken	Force a person to testify against himself or herself

The Individual States

(all 50 of them)

CAN	CAN NOT
Have a militia Create any law they want that isn't prohibited by the Constitution Vote with other States to make amendments, or changes, to the Constitution	Ignore the legal documents of another State Protect a criminal from being put on trial in another State Make a treaty with another country Print money Give titles of nobility Tax imports or exports Create an army Allow slavery Prevent militias or people from owning weapons Force people to house soldiers

Definition:

Militia (noun) - An army of ordinary people, not trained soldiers. They are on call for emergency situations.

<u>Changing the Constitution</u>

The Constitution allows for amendments to be made. An amendment is a change to the rules. If the people decide that the Federal Government needs to be allowed to do something or not allowed to do something, the States can pass an amendment. The new amendment would change the rules for the government.

For example, before the Civil War, the Federal Government was not allowed to make any laws about slavery. As a result, each State decided for itself whether or not to allow slavery. When the Southern States panicked that the Federal Government might make anti-slavery laws even though the rules did not allow it, they tried to leave the United States to start their own country (the Confederacy). These actions led to the Civil War.

When the Civil War ended, the Federal Government was given a new rule: it could ban slavery. This new rule, however, was not the result of the North winning the war. It was not the result of surrender, a treaty, or gunfire. The Federal Government was allowed to make anti-slavery laws only because the States voted to change the rules. The amendment process is the only way that the rules can change.

One of the biggest mistakes people make today is saying that the Constitution is a "living document." Politicians often claim to interpret the Constitution to mean what they want it to mean if they want to make a law that is not permitted or against the rules. It is easier to try to bend the rules than to have the States create new rules.

For example, if the Federal Government wanted to pass a law to make everybody carry a national ID card, there is nothing in the Constitution that allows the Federal Government to do this. Therefore, the Federal Government is not allowed to make everybody carry an ID card. A clever politician may claim that an ID card is necessary for safety and security. This is an example of the Federal Government bending the rules. The rules allow the Federal Government to make laws to defend the country against enemies, but they do not allow the Federal Government to make innocent people carry ID cards. If, however, most of the States believe that an ID card is needed for safety, they could pass an amendment that would then allow the Federal Government to make a law requiring ID cards. Or, each State could individually pass this law.

To summarize, the Federal Government is not allowed to make laws that the rules of the Constitution don't allow. If people think the Federal Government should be allowed to make a law, then an amendment needs to be passed by the States.

The founding fathers warned against the Constitution being interpreted to get laws made that shouldn't be made. They also knew that changes would be necessary, and created a way for those changes to happen. The Constitution is changed when the States pass amendments.

If the States can't agree on a change or do not feel that it's necessary to change the Constitution, they are free to pass individual laws to their liking. For example, you must be 18 to have a full driver's license in New Jersey, but you only have to be 16 to have a full driver's license in South Dakota.

Does the Federal Government Follow the Rules?

This is for you to decide! It is a very important question to ask. When a politician is running to be President, a Senator, or a Representative, you must ask yourself, "Are the laws that he or she wants to make allowed by the Constitution?"

If a President wants to make laws about education, ask yourself "Is the Federal Government allowed to make laws about education? Or is that something that is left to the States?"

If a Senator wants to give money to a troubled company to help them, ask yourself: "Is the Federal Government allowed to give my money away?"

Each time a politician proposes a law, check the Constitution and see if they are allowed to pass such a law. If you think that the government is trying to make a law that it is not allowed to make, then yell at it! Call your Senators and Representatives and tell them that it is against the rules!

You are allowed to tell your government it is doing something wrong. Remember, the government doesn't tell you what to do. You tell the government what to do.

Politicians are very interested in what you think when they are hoping that you will vote for them. Doesn't it make sense to tell them what you think after you've given them the job?

How to Check if a Law Follows the Rules

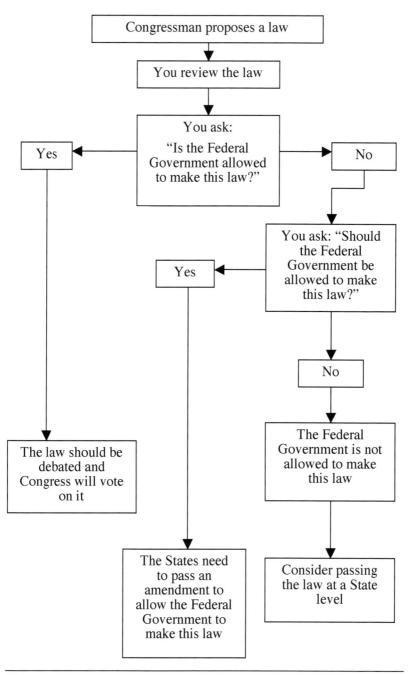

The Constitution in Plain English

Want to know more?

In addition to the rules about what laws can be made, a lot of the Constitution is made up of rules about procedure (how the President is elected, how many Senators there are, etc). We will now look at the entire Constitution, but it has been re-written in plain English. *1

---

[1] The original text of the US Constitution, which begins on page 63, is the source of this edited version of the Constitution.

The Preamble of the Constitution

(A preamble is an introduction. It is a summary of what is to follow. In this case, it explains what the Constitution is going to do.)

The People will form a central government (the Federal Government) in order to makes laws for the States. This is to make sure that the States get along with one another, promise to protect each other from common enemies, protect the people, and make sure that people have freedom. This document will set the rules that the Federal Government and the individual States must follow.

Article 1 – The Legislative Branch

(These rules set up the Legislative Branch of the Federal Government.)

Section 1 – Congress

Congress is the only part of the Federal Government that can make laws. Congress will be made of two parts: the Senate and the House of Representatives.

Section 2 – The House of Representatives

Every two years, the people of each State will elect individuals to be members of the House of Representatives. Representatives must be at least 25 years old, must have been a citizen of the United States for at least 7 years, and must live in the State that they are elected to represent.

A State will elect one person for every 30,000 people in the State. If there are less than 30,000 people in the State, they still elect 1 person to send to the House of Representatives.

> *Example:*
>
> If a State has 90,000 people, they will send 3 representatives. 90,000 divided by 30,000 = 3.

If a member of the House of Representatives quits, gets another job, dies, or leaves their job for any reason, the Governor of the State must hold a vote to select a replacement.

The House of Representatives can vote to impeach an official of the Federal Government.

> Definition:
> Impeach (verb) – to accuse a public official of bad behavior or a crime

One member of the House of Representatives will be picked to be Speaker of the House.

Section 3 - The Senate

Each State elects 2 Senators.   A term in the Senate lasts 6 years.

The election of Senators must be staggered.   In other words, the entire Senate is not replaced at the same time.

> Example:
>
> In one year, 33 Senate seats are voted upon. Two years later, the next 33 Senate seats are voted upon. After another two years, the final 34 seats are voted upon.

If a Senator leaves the job for any reason, the Governor of the State will choose a replacement.

A Senator must be at least 30 years old, must have been a citizen of the United States for at least 9 years, and must live in the State that he or she is elected to represent.

Example:

When Hillary Clinton wanted to be a Senator from New York in 2000, she was not a resident of New York. She moved to New York in 1999 in order to be eligible to be elected to represent New York.

The Vice President will cast a tie-breaking vote if the Senate votes and there is a tie. If there isn't a tie, then the Vice President does not vote.

If there is no Vice President, or the Vice President has to take over for the President, the Senators will choose someone to replace him (this is called a "president pro tempore").

If the House voted to impeach a Federal official, the Senate may vote to convict the accused person. 66% of the Senators must vote for the conviction in order to remove the person from office.

The Senate can remove an elected official, including the President, from their job and make them unable to hold elected office ever again. The Senate cannot put someone on trial in criminal court. For example, if the Senate removes the President, they cannot send him to jail. All they can do is take his job away.

However, an impeached person may then be put on trial in criminal court and face more punishment.

Section 4 – Elections and Meetings

Each State will set rules for electing its Senators and Representatives. Congress can pass laws setting rules that all the States must follow.

The Senators and the Representatives must meet at least once a year on the first Monday in December. They can decide to meet another day, as long as they meet once a year.

(This rule was changed by the 20th amendment. See page 55)

Section 5 – Meeting Rules

The Senators and the Representatives can decide if the election of one of their members was done in an illegal way.

Half of the Senators or half of the Representatives must be present to conduct business.

If less than half of the members of either the Senate or the House of Representatives are present, the present members can force the absent members to show up by threatening them with penalties.

The Senate and the House of Representatives will create rules for how to conduct meetings. They can also kick someone out of a meeting if at least 66% of the members vote for it.

Both the Senate and the House will publish records of their votes unless they think it must be secret.

Neither the Senate nor the House can take a break for longer than three days or change the location where they meet without the approval of the other.

Section 6 – Compensation

The Senators and Representatives will be paid for their work.

They cannot be arrested while they hold office, unless it's for treason, a felony, or disturbing the peace.

> *Example:*
>
> Without this rule, Senators and Representatives might be arrested by their political enemies to prevent them from voting.

You cannot be a Senator or a Representative and hold any other government office at the same time.

Section 7 - Revenue Bills, Legislative Process, Presidential Veto

The House is the first body of Congress to vote for bills that raise money. The Senate can then approve the House's bill, pass it with changes, or reject it.

> *Definition:*
>
> Bill (noun) – a proposal for a law that has not yet been voted on and signed by the President

If the House of Representatives and the Senate both pass a bill, the President can either approve it or veto it.

> *Definition:*
>
> Veto (verb) – when the President prevents a bill from becoming law, even after the House and the Senate passed it

If the President vetoes a bill, the Senate and the House of Representatives can vote on the bill again. In the second vote, if 66% of both the Senators and Representatives vote for the bill, then they can override the President's veto and the bill will become law anyway.

When Congress is in session, if the President doesn't approve or veto a bill within 10 days of receiving it, the bill will become law.

When Congress is not in session, if the President doesn't approve or veto a bill within 10 days of receiving it, the bill will not become law.

Section 8 – What Congress Can Do

The House and the Senate CAN vote to do only the following:

- Collect taxes (as long as all States are taxed equally)
- Pay debts
- Make laws to defend the United States
- Borrow money
- Regulate business between the States
- Make rules about immigration and how someone becomes a citizen
- Make laws about bankruptcy
- Print money and regulate it
- Make laws to punish people who make fake money
- Create post offices and roads to allow mail to be delivered
- Create rules to protect inventors and artists against people who might steal their ideas
- Create lower courts
- Make laws to punish pirates, and anyone who does something wrong to another country
- Declare war on another country, make laws about war, and permit private citizens to seize goods abroad without declaring war

- Raise money for the army, but for only two years at a time
- Create a navy
- Create laws for running the army and navy
- Call on the individual State's militias to help keep peace inside the United States
- Give training to the individual States' militias and appoint officers
- Make laws for the place where the Federal Government conducts business (today, this is Washington DC)
- Make any other laws needed to carry out powers that the government has received from this document

Section 9 – What Congress Can Not Do

The House and Senate CAN NOT do the following:

- Ban people from moving to the United States before 1808
- Allow people to be arrested if they are not charged with a crime
- Punish someone today for an illegal act if the act was committed before it was made illegal
- Pass any direct taxation on the people *(This rule was changed by the 16th amendment. See page 54)*

- Tax goods that go from one State to another
- Treat the States unequally when regulating trade
- Take money from the Treasury without passing a law and keeping a public record of what it does with the money
- Grant people titles of nobility

Section 10 – What the States Can Not Do

Individual States CAN NOT do the following:

- Make a treaty or alliance with another country
- Make their own money
- Grant people titles of nobility
- Tax imports or exports without Congress's permission
- Create an army in peace time, unless they are attacked and are in immediate danger
- Permit private citizens to seize goods abroad

Article 2 - The Executive Branch

(These rules set up the Executive Branch of the Federal Government. The President is the leader of the Executive Branch.)

Section 1 - The President

There will be a President and a Vice President who will serve for four years each time that they are elected.

Each State must choose people to be Electors. The number of Electors is equal to the total number of Senators and Representatives that the State has.

The Electors will vote for the President. Each Elector casts 2 votes. If nobody has a majority (more than 50% of the votes), the House of Representatives will elect someone out of the top five people. If there is a tie for President, the House of Representatives will vote to break the tie.

(This rule was changed by the 12th amendment. See page 51)

The person who finishes 2nd in the Presidential election will become the Vice President.

(This rule was changed by the 12th amendment. See page 51)

Congress will determine when the voting happens.

Only people who were born as citizens of the United States, older than 35, and have lived in the country for 14 years are allowed to be President.

If the President is removed from office, dies, or quits, the Vice President shall become the President. If both the Vice President and the President are removed from office, Congress will pick someone to be President.

(This rule was changed by the 20th and 25th amendments. See pages 55 and 57)

The President will get paid for his job, but his salary cannot be changed while he is President.

Before taking office, the President must take this Oath:

"I do solemnly swear (or affirm) that I will faithfully execute the Office of President of the United States, and will to the best of my ability, preserve, protect and defend the Constitution of the United States."

Section 2 – Presidential Powers

The President will be in charge of the army, the navy, and all of the State militias.

The President has the power to pardon people.

> *Definition:*
>
> Pardon (verb) – to prevent someone from being punished for a crime

The President has the power to propose treaties, but 66% of the Senate must approve any treaty he proposes in order for it to become law.

The President gets to appoint ambassadors, public ministers, Supreme Court judges, and any other positions necessary, but the Senate has to approve the appointments.

If the Senate is not in session, the President can make appointments without the Senate's approval, but when the Senate is back in session, they must approve his appointments.

Section 3 - State of the Union

The President must address Congress to recommend policies and laws which he thinks are a priority (historically, this is the State of the Union address which typically occurs in January).

Section 4 – Removal From Office

The President, Vice President, or any officers of the United States will be removed from office if impeached for and convicted of treason, bribery or other high crimes and misdemeanors.

Article 3 - The Judicial Branch

(These rules set up the Judicial Branch, or the Courts. Specifically, it says what the Supreme Court is and how it interacts with lower courts.)

Section 1 - Judicial Powers

There must be a single Supreme Court that will act as the most powerful court in the country. Judges shall hold their terms as long as they act responsibly, and they will be paid.

There will be lower courts that have judicial authority, but the Supreme Court can overrule their decisions.

Section 2 – Supreme Court Cases, Appeals, Where Trials Are Held

The Judicial Branch will judge all cases about:

- Whether or not Congress's laws follow the rules of the Constitution
- Whether or not the States' laws follow the rules of the Constitution
- Whether treaties are legal and follow the rules of the Constitution
- Controversies with ambassadors, public ministers, disagreements in which the United States is a party, disagreements between States, disagreements between

citizens, disagreements between citizens and foreign countries

In all other matters, the Supreme Court will only get involved if there is an appeal.

Definition:

Appeal (verb) - to apply to a higher court to review a case or issue decided by a lower court

---

Example:

If people believe that a court in Oregon made the wrong decision, they can appeal to the Supreme Court and the Supreme Court can either agree with the original court decision or make a new decision.

If an individual commits a crime, the trial will be held in the State where the crime was committed. If the crime was not committed within a State, then Congress will decide where the trial will be held.

Section 3 - Treason

Treason against the United States is defined as helping the enemy in their fight against the United States.

> *Example:*
>
> In the past, disagreeing with the king or opposing his policies could be considered treason. The Constitution defines treason not as a difference of opinion or expressing an opinion, but actually threatening the country.

You can only be convicted of treason if two people are witnesses to you committing the act of treason, or if you admit to doing it!

Congress will decide the punishment for treason.

Article 4 - The States

(These rules are those that a State must follow if it wants to be one of the United States)

Section 1 – Full Faith and Credit

Each State has to recognize the records and rulings of every other State. Congress will decide how a State can prove its records.

Examples:

If you get married in Wisconsin, when you go to Idaho, Idaho has to recognize you as married!

If you get a driver's license in California, you are allowed to drive in Nebraska. Nebraska can't say you are not allowed to drive in Nebraska because you don't have a Nebraska driver's license.

Section 2 - State Citizens, Extradition

People are entitled to the same freedoms in every State.

If you commit a crime in a State and flee, you will be returned to the State where the crime was committed.

> *Example:*
>
> If you rob a bank in South Carolina and run away to Arkansas to avoid being arrested, a police officer in Arkansas can arrest you and you will be sent back to South Carolina to be put on trial (this is called extradition).

Section 3 - New States

Congress can allow new States to join the United States, but a new State cannot be formed from one or two current States unless the States involved agree and Congress approves.

> *Examples:*
>
> Hawaii is made up of several different islands. A single island couldn't decide to become a separate state, unless all of Hawaii and Congress says OK.
>
> Also, if people on the border of Texas and Oklahoma decide to make their own state, then Texas, Oklahoma, and Congress would have to agree.

Congress will set rules about governing territories and other properties of the United States (land that the United States owns, but are not States).

> *Example:*
>
> Puerto Rico is a United States territory. It is not a State, but it has some protections as a result of being a territory of the United States. People in Puerto Rico pay Social Security tax, but not income tax. They receive some federal aid, but cannot vote for President.

Section 4 - State Government

Each State must have a government run by elected officials, including a legislature and an executive (the governor).

<u>Article 5 – Amendment</u>

(These rules explain how amendments, or changes, are made to the Constitution. This is how new rules are created.)

Changes to the Constitution can be proposed if 66% of Congress decide it's necessary or if 66% of the States think it's necessary. If there is talk of a change (or amendment), a convention will be put together and States will send representatives.

If 3 out of 4 States vote to change the Constitution, then there will be a new rule.

Article 6 - Debts, Supremacy, Oaths

(These rules do three things: first, they explain how money owed before the Constitution was written still needs to be paid back. Second, they explain that the Constitution is the supreme law of the land. Third, they explain the oaths that elected officials must take when they get into office.)

All debts that the United States owes before this Constitution is signed, the United States still has to pay back.

The States must follow laws made by the Federal Government, provided that the laws are allowed by the rules of the Constitution.

All Senators and Representatives, as well as people elected to State government, must take an oath to follow the rules of the Constitution.

Government officials must not be required to take a religious oath.

Article 7 - Ratification Documents

(This section is a record of the States agreeing to the rules.)

Nine of the original States agreed to this Constitution, so it will be the rules from this point forward. On September 17th, 1787, the following representatives from the individual States signed this agreement:

George Washington - President and deputy from Virginia

New Hampshire - John Langdon, Nicholas Gilman

Massachusetts - Nathaniel Gorham, Rufus King

Connecticut - Wm Saml Johnson, Roger Sherman

New York - Alexander Hamilton

New Jersey - Wil Livingston, David Brearley, Wm Paterson, Jona. Dayton

Pennsylvania - B Franklin, Thomas Mifflin, Robt Morris, Geo. Clymer, Thos FitzSimons, Jared Ingersoll, James Wilson, Gouv Morris

Delaware - Geo. Read, Gunning Bedford jun, John Dickinson, Richard Bassett, Jaco. Broom

Maryland - James McHenry, Dan of St Tho Jenifer, Danl Carroll

Virginia - John Blair, James Madison Jr.

North Carolina - Wm Blount, Richd Dobbs Spaight, Hu Williamson

South Carolina - J. Rutledge, Charles Cotesworth Pinckney, Charles Pinckney, Pierce Butler

Georgia - William Few, Abr Baldwin

Attest: William Jackson, Secretary

Amendments (Changes) to the Constitution

(These are the amendments, or new rules, that were made to the Constitution after the States agreed to the original document.)

The first ten amendments are commonly known as the Bill of Rights. They are amendments that list the rights of people that the government cannot take away.

Amendment 1 - Freedom of Religion, Press, Expression

Made a rule on December 15, 1791

Congress cannot pass any law that restricts people from practicing their religion, saying what they want, writing what they want, gathering together in groups, asking their government to do something, or complaining to the government.

Amendment 2 - Right to Bear Arms

Made a rule on December 15, 1791

The States can have militias and cannot stop people from owning weapons.

Amendment 3 - Quartering of Soldiers

Made a rule on December 15, 1791

In peacetime, Congress cannot pass a law forcing people to put soldiers up in their homes.

> *Example:*
>
> In colonial times, the British forced the colonists to allow soldiers to live in their private homes. This amendment makes sure that this doesn't happen.

Amendment 4 - Search and Seizure

Made a rule on December 15, 1791

The Government cannot take or search a person's properties, belongings, or records without a good reason and a warrant.

> *Definition:*
>
> Warrant (noun) – authority from a judge that allows an official to make a search, seizure, or arrest or to execute a judgment

Amendment 5 - Trial and Punishment, Compensation for Takings

Made a rule on December 15, 1791

People are only required to testify in court if a Grand Jury forces them to, if the case is about the army, or during times of war.

> *Definition:*
>
> Grand Jury (noun) – a jury of citizens that decides whether or not there is enough evidence to put a person on trial

The Government cannot put a person on trial for the same reason twice.

The Government cannot force a person to testify against oneself. This is where the expression "I take the fifth" comes from. Referring to the Fifth Amendment, you don't have to answer a question if it will get you in trouble.

The government can't take any of your property without paying you for it.

Amendment 6 - Right to Speedy Trial, Double Jeopardy, Witnesses

Made a rule on December 15, 1791

The Government must provide an accused person with a speedy and public trial in the State where the person is accused of a crime.

People have the right to face the person(s) accusing them of the crime.

The government must allow the accused person to have witnesses come to court and testify in their defense.

Amendment 7 - Trial by Jury in Civil Cases

Made a rule on December 15, 1791

A jury will decide a civil case in which the value of the dispute is greater than $20.

Definition:

Civil Case (noun) – a dispute in which no crime has been committed, such as compensating an injured person, enforcing a contract, or paying for damaged property

---

Amendment 8 - Cruel and Unusual Punishment

Made a rule on December 15, 1791

If a person is arrested, the government cannot require them to post excessive bail, or punish them cruelly if convicted.

Definition:

Bail (noun) – a sum of money exchanged for the release of an arrested person as a guarantee of that person's appearance for trial

---

Amendment 9 – Other Rights

Made a rule on December 15, 1791

Lawmakers cannot use the Constitution as a way to limit the freedoms of people. Any rights that people have must be respected, even if those rights are not listed in the Constitution.

> *Example:*
>
> You may hear people claim a "right to privacy." Although the Constitution never mentions a right to privacy, some people argue that it is implied here.

Amendment 10 - Powers of the States and People

Made a rule on December 15, 1791

If this Constitution doesn't explicitly say that the Federal Government can do something, then the Federal Government is not allowed to do it! Only the States or the people are allowed to do it!

> *Example:*
>
> In 1979, The Federal Government created the Department of Education. You can argue that this was against the rules since nothing in the Constitution says the Federal Government is allowed to make laws about education and that only States should make education laws.

Amendment 11 - Judicial Limits

Made a rule on February 7, 1795

The judicial system may not permit people or citizens of foreign countries to file lawsuits against a State in Federal court.

> Example:
>
> A person in West Virginia cannot sue the State of Alabama. Alabama, if forced to pay, would have to tax its people to get the money. This would not be fair to the citizens of Alabama.

Amendment 12 - Choosing the President, Vice-President

Made a rule on June 15, 1804

This amendment changed the rules that Electors follow to choose the President and Vice President. Instead of getting two votes, each Elector now gets one vote. They cast separate votes for President and Vice President.

If no Presidential candidate gets a majority of votes, the House picks a President from the top three candidates, instead of the top five.

If no Vice Presidential candidate gets a majority of votes, the Senate picks a Vice President from the top two candidates.

If a President cannot be chosen, a Vice President chosen by the Senate can serve as President until a President is elected.

You cannot be Vice President if you are not eligible to be President.

Amendment 13 - Slavery Abolished

Made a rule on December 6, 1865

Slavery and forced servitude is not allowed in any State.

Amendment 14 - Citizenship Rights

Made a rule on July 9, 1868

A person born in the United States is automatically a citizen.

When deciding how many representatives a State gets to send to the House, everyone must be counted as an individual. This was to stop a rule that counted slaves as 3/5 people.

> *Example:*
>
> Before this change, if a State had 50,000 slaves, they would only count 30,000 toward the State's total population when calculating how many representatives a State received. This was a compromise between the North, which had few slaves, and the South, which had many. While most Southerners were reluctant to give slaves rights, it was convenient to have them count when deciding how much say their State had in the House of Representatives.

A Confederate in the Civil War cannot be a Senator, Representative, President, Vice President, a military officer, or a member of State Government. However, if 66% of Congress decides to make an exception, then it is allowed.

The United States will not have to pay the debts that Confederate States owe. These debts are declared illegal.

> *Example:*
>
> Some Southern States took loans from French banks to help pay for the Civil War. The United States will not be responsible for paying back these loans.

Nobody can demand repayment for the loss of a slave.

> *Example:*
>
> If you owned a slave at the time that slavery was made illegal, you can't demand money for lost property.

Amendment 15 – Voting Rights for All Races

Made a rule on February 3, 1870

The Government cannot stop someone from voting because of race or ethnicity, or because they used to be a slave.

Amendment 16 – Income Tax

Made a rule on February 3, 1913

Congress has the right to tax incomes.

Amendment 17 - Senators Elected by Popular Vote

Made a rule on April 8, 1913

Instead of State legislatures picking the Senators, the people of the State will directly vote for their Senators. Once elected, a Senator serves a term of 6 years.

If a Senator leaves office or dies, the Governor picks a replacement.

Amendment 18 - Prohibition

Made a rule on January 16, 1919

Congress can make laws that make alcohol illegal (beer, wine, liquor of any kind).

Amendment 19 – Voting Rights for Women

Made a rule on August 18, 1920

The Government cannot stop women from voting.

Amendment 20 - Presidential, Congressional Terms

Made a rule on January 23, 1933

The new President and Vice President will take over at noon on January 20th.

The new Senators and Representatives will take over at noon on January 3rd.

Congress must meet at least once a year on January 3rd, unless they decide to pick another day.

If the President dies in the time between the election and the day he takes office, the Vice President will become President instead.

Amendment 21 - Prohibition Repealed

Made a rule on December 5, 1933

The 18th Amendment is no longer a rule. Congress can no longer create laws that make alcohol illegal.

Amendment 22 - Presidential Term Limits

Made a rule on February 27, 1951

Nobody can be elected President more than twice. If a person is President for more than 2 years without having been elected President (if the previous President resigns, for example), then they can only be elected one more time.

Amendment 23 - Presidential Vote for Washington DC

Made a rule on March 29, 1961

Washington DC is allowed to send Electors to vote for President. The number of Electors they get is the same as whichever State has the fewest electors.

> *Example:*
>
> The least populated States, Alaska, Delaware, South Dakota, North Dakota, Montana, Vermont, and Wyoming, each have 3 electoral votes. Therefore, Washington DC gets 3 electoral votes.
>
> *(as of the 2008 Presidential election)*

Amendment 24 – No Poll Taxes

Made a rule on January 23, 1964

There cannot be a tax to vote. The Government can't prevent people from voting by making them pay money to vote.

Amendment 25 - Presidential Disability and Succession

Made a rule on February 10, 1967

If the President is removed from office, quits his job, or dies, the Vice President becomes President.

The new President must appoint a Vice President (before this amendment, there were times when Vice Presidents became President and did not appoint a new Vice President).

If either the President or the Vice President and a majority of executive officers believe that the President has become unable to do his job, Congress may be asked to transfer presidential powers to the Vice President.

The President, when able to do his job again, can ask Congress to return his power.

> *Example:*
>
> In 2002 and 2007, President George W. Bush transferred his presidential power to Vice President Dick Cheney when undergoing medical procedures that required him to be asleep.

Amendment 26 – Minimum Voting Age

Made a rule on July 1, 1971

The Government cannot stop a person from voting because of age, if they are 18 or older.

Amendment 27 - Limiting Congressional Pay Increases

Made a rule on May 7, 1992

How much Senators and Representatives are paid can only be changed after an election of Representatives.

What's Not in the Constitution?

Now that you've read the rules, you may have noticed some things that are not in the Constitution. This is the tricky part. You have to decide whether laws follow the rules or not. There isn't always a right and wrong answer.

Consider these questions:

Is the Federal Government allowed to make laws about education? Yes or No?

Is the Federal Government allowed to create a central bank, like the Federal Reserve? Yes or No?

Is the Federal Government allowed to "bail out" companies that are in financial trouble? Yes or No?

Is the Federal Government allowed to force people to join the army (this is called a draft)? Yes or No?

Is the Federal Government allowed to give people money (this is called welfare)? Yes or No?

Is the Federal Government allowed to bribe the States with funding to get them to pass laws (such as a minimum drinking age)? Yes or No?

Is the Federal Government allowed to buy mortgages (with government controlled companies such as Fannie Mae and Freddie Mac)? Yes or No?

Is the Federal Government allowed to create programs like Social Security? Yes or No?

Remember, there may be no clear answer to some of these. You may also not like the answer.

You may think that Social Security is a good thing. Your friend may point out that there is no rule that allows the Federal Government to create Social Security. Both of you may be right. Maybe there should be an amendment, or a change in the rules, to allow Social Security.

> *Definition:*
>
> Social Security (noun) – a federal program where workers' income is involuntarily taxed and the money is given to help retired or disabled people

You may disagree with other people, and that's okay. The important thing is that you discuss the laws and decide for yourself if your government is following the rules.

The laws that the government makes will affect your life. You need to stay educated about what the government is doing and make sure it is doing what it is allowed to do.

The Individual's Duty

There is an excerpt from The Declaration of Independence on Page 4 of this book. In it, Thomas Jefferson basically says that when the government abuses its power or breaks the rules, it is up to the people to remove and replace the government with a better one.

When Thomas Jefferson wrote this, he was referring to the King of England. Because the rules of Great Britain didn't allow for the people to protest their government, the only way for the people to change their government was through war.

Luckily, the rules of our government allow the people to protest and to replace their government by voting new individuals into office.

The King of England was the boss of the people. However, we are the bosses of the government.

Remember, elected officials work for YOU. You are the boss. If they aren't doing their job, it is up to you to tell them to do their job correctly.

The Original Text of the US Constitution

(This is provided as the book's primary source and because everyone should have a copy.)

We the People of the United States, in Order to form a more perfect Union, establish Justice, insure domestic Tranquility, provide for the common defence, promote the general Welfare, and secure the Blessings of Liberty to ourselves and our Posterity, do ordain and establish this Constitution for the United States of America.

Article. I.

Section. 1. All legislative Powers herein granted shall be vested in a Congress of the United States, which shall consist of a Senate and House of Representatives.

Section. 2. The House of Representatives shall be composed of Members chosen every second Year by the People of the several States, and the Electors in each State shall have the Qualifications requisite for Electors of the most numerous Branch of the State Legislature.

No Person shall be a Representative who shall not have attained to the Age of twenty five Years, and been seven Years a Citizen of the United States, and who shall not, when elected, be an Inhabitant of that State in which he shall be chosen.

Representatives and direct Taxes shall be apportioned among the several States which may be included within this Union, according to their respective Numbers, which shall be determined by adding to the whole Number of free Persons, including those bound to Service for a Term of Years, and excluding Indians not taxed, three fifths of all other Persons. The actual Enumeration shall be made within three Years after the first Meeting of the Congress of the United States, and within every subsequent Term of ten Years, in such Manner as they shall by Law direct. The Number of Representatives shall not exceed one for every thirty Thousand, but each State shall have at Least one Representative; and until such enumeration shall be made, the State of New Hampshire shall be entitled to chuse three, Massachusetts eight, Rhode-Island and Providence Plantations one, Connecticut five, New-York six, New Jersey four, Pennsylvania eight, Delaware one, Maryland six, Virginia ten, North Carolina five, South Carolina five, and Georgia three.

When vacancies happen in the Representation from any State, the Executive Authority thereof shall issue Writs of Election to fill such Vacancies.

The House of Representatives shall chuse their Speaker and other Officers; and shall have the sole Power of Impeachment.

Section. 3. The Senate of the United States shall be composed of two Senators from each State, chosen by the Legislature thereof, for six Years; and each Senator shall have one Vote.

Immediately after they shall be assembled in Consequence of the first Election, they shall be divided as equally as may be into three Classes. The Seats of the Senators of the first Class shall be vacated at the Expiration of the second Year, of the second Class at the Expiration of the fourth Year, and of the third Class at the Expiration of the sixth Year, so that one third may be chosen every second Year; and if Vacancies happen by Resignation, or otherwise, during the Recess of the Legislature of any State, the Executive thereof may make temporary Appointments until the next Meeting of the Legislature, which shall then fill such Vacancies.

No Person shall be a Senator who shall not have attained to the Age of thirty Years, and been nine Years a Citizen of the United States, and who shall not, when elected, be an Inhabitant of that State for which he shall be chosen.

The Vice President of the United States shall be President of the Senate, but shall have no Vote, unless they be equally divided.

The Senate shall chuse their other Officers, and also a President pro tempore, in the Absence of the Vice President, or when he shall exercise the Office of President of the United States.

The Senate shall have the sole Power to try all Impeachments. When sitting for that Purpose, they shall be on Oath or Affirmation. When the President of the United States is tried, the Chief Justice shall preside: And no Person shall be convicted without the Concurrence of two thirds of the Members present.

Judgment in Cases of Impeachment shall not extend further than to removal from Office, and disqualification to hold and enjoy any Office of honor, Trust or Profit under the United States: but the Party convicted shall nevertheless be liable and subject to Indictment, Trial, Judgment and Punishment, according to Law.

Section. 4. The Times, Places and Manner of holding Elections for Senators and Representatives, shall be prescribed in each State by the Legislature thereof; but the Congress may at any time by Law make or alter such Regulations, except as to the Places of chusing Senators.

The Congress shall assemble at least once in every Year, and such Meeting shall be on the first Monday in December, unless they shall by Law appoint a different Day.

Section. 5. Each House shall be the Judge of the Elections, Returns and Qualifications of its own Members, and a Majority of each shall constitute a Quorum to do Business; but a smaller Number may adjourn from day to day, and may be authorized to compel the Attendance of absent Members, in such Manner, and under such Penalties as each House may provide.

Each House may determine the Rules of its Proceedings, punish its Members for disorderly Behaviour, and, with the Concurrence of two thirds, expel a Member.

Each House shall keep a Journal of its Proceedings, and from time to time publish the same, excepting such Parts as may in their Judgment require Secrecy; and the Yeas and Nays of the Members of either House on any question shall, at the Desire of one fifth of those Present, be entered on the Journal.

Neither House, during the Session of Congress, shall, without the Consent of the other, adjourn for more than three days, nor to any other Place than that in which the two Houses shall be sitting.

Section. 6. The Senators and Representatives shall receive a Compensation for their Services, to be ascertained by Law, and paid out of the Treasury of the United States. They shall in all Cases, except Treason, Felony and Breach of the Peace, be privileged from Arrest during their Attendance at the Session of their respective Houses, and in going to and returning from the same; and for any Speech or Debate in either House, they shall not be questioned in any other Place.

No Senator or Representative shall, during the Time for which he was elected, be appointed to any civil Office under the Authority of the United States, which shall have been created, or the Emoluments whereof shall have been encreased during such time; and no Person holding any Office under the United States, shall be a Member of either House during his Continuance in Office.

Section. 7. All Bills for raising Revenue shall originate in the House of Representatives; but the Senate may propose or concur with Amendments as on other Bills.

Every Bill which shall have passed the House of Representatives and the Senate, shall, before it become a Law, be presented to the

President of the United States; If he approve he shall sign it, but if not he shall return it, with his Objections to that House in which it shall have originated, who shall enter the Objections at large on their Journal, and proceed to reconsider it. If after such Reconsideration two thirds of that House shall agree to pass the Bill, it shall be sent, together with the Objections, to the other House, by which it shall likewise be reconsidered, and if approved by two thirds of that House, it shall become a Law. But in all such Cases the Votes of both Houses shall be determined by yeas and Nays, and the Names of the Persons voting for and against the Bill shall be entered on the Journal of each House respectively. If any Bill shall not be returned by the President within ten Days (Sundays excepted) after it shall have been presented to him, the Same shall be a Law, in like Manner as if he had signed it, unless the Congress by their Adjournment prevent its Return, in which Case it shall not be a Law.

Every Order, Resolution, or Vote to which the Concurrence of the Senate and House of Representatives may be necessary (except on a question of Adjournment) shall be presented to the President of the United States; and before the Same shall take Effect, shall be approved by him, or being disapproved by him, shall be repassed by two thirds of the Senate and House of Representatives, according to the Rules and Limitations prescribed in the Case of a Bill.

Section. 8. The Congress shall have Power To lay and collect Taxes, Duties, Imposts and Excises, to pay the Debts and provide for the common Defence and general Welfare of the United States; but all Duties, Imposts and Excises shall be uniform throughout the United States;

To borrow Money on the credit of the United States;

To regulate Commerce with foreign Nations, and among the several States, and with the Indian Tribes;

To establish an uniform Rule of Naturalization, and uniform Laws on the subject of Bankruptcies throughout the United States;

To coin Money, regulate the Value thereof, and of foreign Coin, and fix the Standard of Weights and Measures;

To provide for the Punishment of counterfeiting the Securities and current Coin of the United States;

To establish Post Offices and post Roads;

To promote the Progress of Science and useful Arts, by securing for limited Times to Authors and Inventors the exclusive Right to their respective Writings and Discoveries;

To constitute Tribunals inferior to the supreme Court;

To define and punish Piracies and Felonies committed on the high Seas, and Offences against the Law of Nations;

To declare War, grant Letters of Marque and Reprisal, and make Rules concerning Captures on Land and Water;

To raise and support Armies, but no Appropriation of Money to that Use shall be for a longer Term than two Years;

To provide and maintain a Navy;

To make Rules for the Government and Regulation of the land and naval Forces;

To provide for calling forth the Militia to execute the Laws of the Union, suppress Insurrections and repel Invasions;

To provide for organizing, arming, and disciplining, the Militia, and for governing such Part of them as may be employed in the Service of the United States, reserving to the States respectively, the Appointment of the Officers, and the Authority of training the Militia according to the discipline prescribed by Congress;

To exercise exclusive Legislation in all Cases whatsoever, over such District (not exceeding ten Miles square) as may, by Cession of particular States, and the Acceptance of Congress, become the Seat of the Government of the United States, and to exercise like Authority over all Places purchased by the Consent of the Legislature of the State in which the Same shall be, for the Erection of Forts, Magazines, Arsenals, dock-Yards, and other needful Buildings; — And

To make all Laws which shall be necessary and proper for carrying into Execution the foregoing Powers, and all other Powers vested by this Constitution in the Government of the United States, or in any Department or Officer thereof.

Section. 9. The Migration or Importation of such Persons as any of the States now existing shall think proper to admit, shall not be prohibited by the Congress prior to the Year one thousand eight hundred and eight, but a Tax or duty may be imposed on such Importation, not exceeding ten dollars for each Person.

The Privilege of the Writ of Habeas Corpus shall not be suspended, unless when in Cases of Rebellion or Invasion the public Safety may require it.

No Bill of Attainder or ex post facto Law shall be passed.

No Capitation, or other direct, Tax shall be laid, unless in Proportion to the Census or Enumeration herein before directed to be taken.

No Tax or Duty shall be laid on Articles exported from any State.

No Preference shall be given by any Regulation of Commerce or Revenue to the Ports of one State over those of another; nor shall Vessels bound to, or from, one State, be obliged to enter, clear, or pay Duties in another.

No Money shall be drawn from the Treasury, but in Consequence of Appropriations made by Law; and a regular Statement and Account of the Receipts and Expenditures of all public Money shall be published from time to time.

No Title of Nobility shall be granted by the United States: And no Person holding any Office of Profit or Trust under them, shall, without the Consent of the Congress, accept of any present, Emolument, Office, or Title, of any kind whatever, from any King, Prince, or foreign State.

Section. 10. No State shall enter into any Treaty, Alliance, or Confederation; grant Letters of Marque and Reprisal; coin Money; emit Bills of Credit; make any Thing but gold and silver Coin a Tender in Payment of Debts; pass any Bill of Attainder, ex post facto Law, or Law impairing the Obligation of Contracts, or grant any Title of Nobility.

No State shall, without the Consent of the Congress, lay any Imposts or Duties on Imports or Exports, except what may be absolutely necessary for executing it's inspection Laws; and the net Produce of all Duties and Imposts, laid by any State on Imports or Exports, shall be for the Use of the Treasury of the United States; and all such Laws shall be subject to the Revision and Controul of the Congress.

No State shall, without the Consent of Congress, lay any Duty of Tonnage, keep Troops, or Ships of War in time of Peace, enter into any Agreement or Compact with another State, or with a foreign Power, or engage in War, unless actually invaded, or in such imminent Danger as will not admit of delay.

Article. II

Section. 1. The executive Power shall be vested in a President of the United States of America. He shall hold his Office during the Term of four Years, and, together with the Vice President, chosen for the same Term, be elected, as follows:

Each State shall appoint, in such Manner as the Legislature thereof may direct, a Number of Electors, equal to the whole Number of Senators and Representatives to which the State may be entitled in the Congress: but no Senator or Representative, or Person holding an Office of Trust or Profit under the United States, shall be appointed an Elector.

The Electors shall meet in their respective States, and vote by Ballot for two Persons, of whom one at least shall not be an Inhabitant of the same State with themselves. And they shall make a List of all the Persons voted for, and of the Number of Votes for each; which List they shall sign and certify, and transmit sealed to the Seat of the Government of the United States, directed to the President of the Senate. The President of the Senate shall, in the Presence of the Senate and House of Representatives, open all the Certificates, and the Votes shall then be counted. The Person having the greatest Number of Votes shall be the President, if such Number be a Majority of the whole Number of Electors appointed; and if there be more than one who have such Majority, and have an equal Number of Votes, then the House of Representatives shall immediately chuse by Ballot one of them for President; and if no Person have a Majority, then from the five highest on the List the said House shall in like Manner chuse the President. But in chusing the President, the Votes shall be taken by States, the Representation from each State having one Vote; a quorum for this Purpose shall consist of a Member or Members from two thirds of the States, and a Majority of all the States shall be necessary to a Choice. In every Case, after the Choice of the President, the Person having the greatest Number of Votes of the Electors shall be the Vice President. But if there should remain two or more who have equal Votes, the Senate shall chuse from them by Ballot the Vice President.

The Congress may determine the Time of chusing the Electors, and the Day on which they shall give their Votes; which Day shall be the same throughout the United States.

No Person except a natural born Citizen, or a Citizen of the United States, at the time of the Adoption of this Constitution, shall be eligible to the Office of President; neither shall any Person be eligible to that Office who shall not have attained to the Age of thirty five Years, and been fourteen Years a Resident within the United States.

In Case of the Removal of the President from Office, or of his Death, Resignation, or Inability to discharge the Powers and Duties of the said Office, the Same shall devolve on the Vice President, and the Congress may by Law provide for the Case of Removal, Death, Resignation or Inability, both of the President and Vice President, declaring what Officer shall then act as President, and such Officer shall act accordingly, until the Disability be removed, or a President shall be elected.

The President shall, at stated Times, receive for his Services, a Compensation, which shall neither be increased nor diminished during the Period for which he shall have been elected, and he shall not receive within that Period any other Emolument from the United States, or any of them.

Before he enter on the Execution of his Office, he shall take the following Oath or Affirmation: — "I do solemnly swear (or affirm) that I will faithfully execute the Office of President of the United States, and will to the best of my Ability, preserve, protect and defend the Constitution of the United States."

Section. 2. The President shall be Commander in Chief of the Army and Navy of the United States, and of the Militia of the several States, when called into the actual Service of the United States; he may require the Opinion, in writing, of the principal Officer in each of the executive Departments, upon any Subject relating to the Duties of their respective Offices, and he shall have Power to grant Reprieves and Pardons for Offences against the United States, except in Cases of Impeachment.

He shall have Power, by and with the Advice and Consent of the Senate, to make Treaties, provided two thirds of the Senators present concur; and he shall nominate, and by and with the Advice and Consent of the Senate, shall appoint Ambassadors, other public Ministers and Consuls, Judges of the supreme Court, and all other Officers of the United States, whose Appointments are not herein otherwise provided for, and which shall be established by Law: but the Congress may by Law vest the Appointment of such inferior Officers, as they think proper, in the President alone, in the Courts of Law, or in the Heads of Departments.

The President shall have Power to fill up all Vacancies that may happen during the Recess of the Senate, by granting Commissions which shall expire at the End of their next Session.

Section. 3. He shall from time to time give to the Congress Information of the State of the Union, and recommend to their Consideration such Measures as he shall judge necessary and expedient; he may, on extraordinary Occasions, convene both Houses, or either of them, and in Case of Disagreement between them, with Respect to the Time of Adjournment, he may adjourn them to such Time as he shall think proper; he shall receive Ambassadors and other public Ministers; he shall take Care that the

Laws be faithfully executed, and shall Commission all the Officers of the United States.

Section. 4. The President, Vice President and all civil Officers of the United States, shall be removed from Office on Impeachment for, and Conviction of, Treason, Bribery, or other high Crimes and Misdemeanors.

Article. III.

Section. 1. The judicial Power of the United States shall be vested in one supreme Court, and in such inferior Courts as the Congress may from time to time ordain and establish. The Judges, both of the supreme and inferior Courts, shall hold their Offices during good Behaviour, and shall, at stated Times, receive for their Services a Compensation, which shall not be diminished during their Continuance in Office.

Section. 2. The judicial Power shall extend to all Cases, in Law and Equity, arising under this Constitution, the Laws of the United States, and Treaties made, or which shall be made, under their Authority; — to all Cases affecting Ambassadors, other public Ministers and Consuls; — to all Cases of admiralty and maritime Jurisdiction; — to Controversies to which the United States shall be a Party; — to Controversies between two or more States; — between a State and Citizens of another State; — between Citizens of different States; — between Citizens of the same State claiming Lands under Grants of different States, and between a State, or the Citizens thereof, and foreign States, Citizens or Subjects.

In all Cases affecting Ambassadors, other public Ministers and Consuls, and those in which a State shall be Party, the supreme Court shall have original Jurisdiction. In all the other Cases before mentioned, the supreme Court shall have appellate Jurisdiction, both as to Law and Fact, with such Exceptions, and under such Regulations as the Congress shall make.

The Trial of all Crimes, except in Cases of Impeachment, shall be by Jury; and such Trial shall be held in the State where the said Crimes shall have been committed; but when not committed within any State, the Trial shall be at such Place or Places as the Congress may by Law have directed.

Section. 3. Treason against the United States shall consist only in levying War against them, or in adhering to their Enemies, giving them Aid and Comfort. No Person shall be convicted of Treason unless on the Testimony of two Witnesses to the same overt Act, or on Confession in open Court.

The Congress shall have Power to declare the Punishment of Treason, but no Attainder of Treason shall work Corruption of Blood, or Forfeiture except during the Life of the Person attainted.

Article. IV.

Section. 1. Full Faith and Credit shall be given in each State to the public Acts, Records, and judicial Proceedings of every other State. And the Congress may by general Laws prescribe the Manner in which such Acts, Records and Proceedings shall be proved, and the Effect thereof.

Section. 2. The Citizens of each State shall be entitled to all Privileges and Immunities of Citizens in the several States.

A Person charged in any State with Treason, Felony, or other Crime, who shall flee from Justice, and be found in another State, shall on Demand of the executive Authority of the State from which he fled, be delivered up, to be removed to the State having Jurisdiction of the Crime.

No Person held to Service or Labour in one State, under the Laws thereof, escaping into another, shall, in Consequence of any Law or Regulation therein, be discharged from such Service or Labour, but shall be delivered up on Claim of the Party to whom such Service or Labour may be due.

Section. 3. New States may be admitted by the Congress into this Union; but no new State shall be formed or erected within the Jurisdiction of any other State; nor any State be formed by the Junction of two or more States, or Parts of States, without the Consent of the Legislatures of the States concerned as well as of the Congress.

The Congress shall have Power to dispose of and make all needful Rules and Regulations respecting the Territory or other Property belonging to the United States; and nothing in this Constitution shall be so construed as to Prejudice any Claims of the United States, or of any particular State.

Section. 4. The United States shall guarantee to every State in this Union a Republican Form of Government, and shall protect each of them against Invasion; and on Application of the Legislature, or of the Executive (when the Legislature cannot be convened), against domestic Violence.

Article. V.

The Congress, whenever two thirds of both Houses shall deem it necessary, shall propose Amendments to this Constitution, or, on the Application of the Legislatures of two thirds of the several States, shall call a Convention for proposing Amendments, which, in either Case, shall be valid to all Intents and Purposes, as Part of this Constitution, when ratified by the Legislatures of three fourths of the several States, or by Conventions in three fourths thereof, as the one or the other Mode of Ratification may be proposed by the Congress; Provided that no Amendment which may be made prior to the Year One thousand eight hundred and eight shall in any Manner affect the first and fourth Clauses in the Ninth Section of the first Article; and that no State, without its Consent, shall be deprived of its equal Suffrage in the Senate.

Article. VI.

All Debts contracted and Engagements entered into, before the Adoption of this Constitution, shall be as valid against the United States under this Constitution, as under the Confederation.

This Constitution, and the Laws of the United States which shall be made in Pursuance thereof; and all Treaties made, or which shall be made, under the Authority of the United States, shall be the supreme Law of the Land; and the Judges in every State shall be bound thereby, any Thing in the Constitution or Laws of any State to the Contrary notwithstanding.

The Senators and Representatives before mentioned, and the Members of the several State Legislatures, and all executive and judicial Officers, both of the United States and of the several States, shall be bound by Oath or Affirmation, to support this Constitution; but no religious Test shall ever be required as a Qualification to any Office or public Trust under the United States.

Article VII - Ratification Documents

The Ratification of the Conventions of nine States, shall be sufficient for the Establishment of this Constitution between the States so ratifying the Same.

Done in Convention by the Unanimous Consent of the States present the Seventeenth Day of September in the Year of our Lord one thousand seven hundred and Eighty seven and of the

Independence of the United States of America the Twelfth. In Witness whereof We have hereunto subscribed our Names. Note

Go Washington - President and deputy from Virginia

New Hampshire - John Langdon, Nicholas Gilman

Massachusetts - Nathaniel Gorham, Rufus King

Connecticut - Wm Saml Johnson, Roger Sherman

New York - Alexander Hamilton

New Jersey - Wil Livingston, David Brearley, Wm Paterson, Jona. Dayton

Pensylvania - B Franklin, Thomas Mifflin, Robt Morris, Geo. Clymer, Thos FitzSimons, Jared Ingersoll, James Wilson, Gouv Morris

Delaware - Geo. Read, Gunning Bedford jun, John Dickinson, Richard Bassett, Jaco. Broom

Maryland - James McHenry, Dan of St Tho Jenifer, Danl Carroll

Virginia - John Blair, James Madison Jr.

North Carolina - Wm Blount, Richd Dobbs Spaight, Hu Williamson

South Carolina - J. Rutledge, Charles Cotesworth Pinckney, Charles Pinckney, Pierce Butler

Georgia - William Few, Abr Baldwin

Attest: William Jackson, Secretary

Amendment I

Congress shall make no law respecting an establishment of religion, or prohibiting the free exercise thereof; or abridging the freedom of speech, or of the press; or the right of the people peaceably to assemble, and to petition the Government for a redress of grievances.

Amendment II

A well regulated Militia, being necessary to the security of a free State, the right of the people to keep and bear Arms, shall not be infringed.

Amendement III

No Soldier shall, in time of peace be quartered in any house, without the consent of the Owner, nor in time of war, but in a manner to be prescribed by law.

Amendment IV

The right of the people to be secure in their persons, houses, papers, and effects, against unreasonable searches and seizures, shall not be violated, and no Warrants shall issue, but upon probable cause, supported by Oath or affirmation, and particularly describing the place to be searched, and the persons or things to be seized.

Amendment V

No person shall be held to answer for a capital, or otherwise infamous crime, unless on a presentment or indictment of a Grand Jury, except in cases arising in the land or naval forces, or in the Militia, when in actual service in time of War or public danger; nor shall any person be subject for the same offence to be twice put in jeopardy of life or limb; nor shall be compelled in any criminal case to be a witness against himself, nor be deprived of life, liberty, or property, without due process of law; nor shall private property be taken for public use, without just compensation.

Amendment VI

In all criminal prosecutions, the accused shall enjoy the right to a speedy and public trial, by an impartial jury of the State and district wherein the crime shall have been committed, which district shall have been previously ascertained by law, and to be informed of the nature and cause of the accusation; to be confronted with the witnesses against him; to have compulsory process for obtaining witnesses in his favor, and to have the Assistance of Counsel for his defence.

Amendment VII

In Suits at common law, where the value in controversy shall exceed twenty dollars, the right of trial by jury shall be preserved, and no fact tried by a jury, shall be otherwise re-examined in any Court of the United States, than according to the rules of the common law.

Amendment VIII

Excessive bail shall not be required, nor excessive fines imposed, nor cruel and unusual punishments inflicted.

Amendment IX

The enumeration in the Constitution, of certain rights, shall not be construed to deny or disparage others retained by the people.

Amendment X

The powers not delegated to the United States by the Constitution, nor prohibited by it to the States, are reserved to the States respectively, or to the people.

Amendment XI

The Judicial power of the United States shall not be construed to extend to any suit in law or equity, commenced or prosecuted against one of the United States by Citizens of another State, or by Citizens or Subjects of any Foreign State.

Amendment XII

The Electors shall meet in their respective states, and vote by ballot for President and Vice-President, one of whom, at least, shall not be an inhabitant of the same state with themselves; they shall name in their ballots the person voted for as President, and in distinct ballots the person voted for as Vice-President, and they shall make distinct lists of all persons voted for as President, and of all persons voted for as Vice-President, and of the number of votes for each, which lists they shall sign and certify, and transmit sealed to the seat of the government of the United States, directed to the President of the Senate; — The President of the Senate shall, in the presence of the Senate and House of Representatives, open all the certificates and the votes shall then be counted; — The person having the greatest number of votes for President, shall be the President, if such number be a majority of the whole number of Electors appointed; and if no person have such majority, then from the persons having the highest numbers not exceeding three on the list of those voted for as President, the House of Representatives shall choose immediately, by ballot, the President. But in choosing the President, the votes shall be taken by states, the representation from each state having one vote; a quorum for this purpose shall consist of a member or members from two-thirds of the states, and a majority of all the states shall be necessary to a choice. And if the House of Representatives shall not choose a President whenever the right of choice shall devolve upon them, before the fourth day of March next following, then the Vice-President shall act as President, as in the case of the death or other constitutional disability of the President. — The person having the greatest number of votes as Vice-President, shall be the Vice-President, if such number be a majority of the whole number of Electors appointed, and if no person have a majority, then from the two highest numbers on the list, the Senate shall choose the Vice-President; a quorum for the purpose shall consist of two-thirds of the whole number of Senators, and a majority of the whole number shall be necessary to a choice. But no person constitutionally ineligible to the office of President shall be eligible to that of Vice-President of the United States.

Amendment XIII

Section. 1. Neither slavery nor involuntary servitude, except as a punishment for crime whereof the party shall have been duly convicted, shall exist within the United States, or any place subject to their jurisdiction.

Section. 2. Congress shall have power to enforce this article by appropriate legislation.

Amendment XIV

Section. 1. All persons born or naturalized in the United States, and subject to the jurisdiction thereof, are citizens of the United States and of the State wherein they reside. No State shall make or enforce any law which shall abridge the privileges or immunities of citizens of the United States; nor shall any State deprive any person of life, liberty, or property, without due process of law; nor deny to any person within its jurisdiction the equal protection of the laws.

Section. 2. Representatives shall be apportioned among the several States according to their respective numbers, counting the whole number of persons in each State, excluding Indians not taxed. But when the right to vote at any election for the choice of electors for President and Vice President of the United States, Representatives in Congress, the Executive and Judicial officers of a State, or the members of the Legislature thereof, is denied to any of the male inhabitants of such State, being twenty-one years of age, and citizens of the United States, or in any way abridged, except for participation in rebellion, or other crime, the basis of representation therein shall be reduced in the proportion which the number of such male citizens shall bear to the whole number of male citizens twenty-one years of age in such State.

Section. 3. No person shall be a Senator or Representative in Congress, or elector of President and Vice President, or hold any office, civil or military, under the United States, or under any State, who, having previously taken an oath, as a member of Congress, or as an officer of the United States, or as a member of any State legislature, or as an executive or judicial officer of any State, to support the Constitution of the United States, shall have engaged in insurrection or rebellion against the same, or given aid or comfort to the enemies thereof. But Congress may by a vote of two-thirds of each House, remove such disability.

Section. 4. The validity of the public debt of the United States, authorized by law, including debts incurred for payment of pensions and bounties for services in suppressing insurrection or rebellion, shall not be questioned. But neither the United States nor any State shall assume or pay any debt or obligation incurred in aid of insurrection or rebellion against the United States, or any claim for the loss or emancipation of any slave; but all such debts, obligations and claims shall be held illegal and void.

Section. 5. The Congress shall have power to enforce, by appropriate legislation, the provisions of this article.

Amendment XV

Section. 1. The right of citizens of the United States to vote shall not be denied or abridged by the United States or by any State on account of race, color, or previous condition of servitude.

Section. 2. The Congress shall have power to enforce this article by appropriate legislation.

Amendment XIV

The Congress shall have power to lay and collect taxes on incomes, from whatever source derived, without apportionment among the several States, and without regard to any census or enumeration.

Amendment XVII

The Senate of the United States shall be composed of two Senators from each State, elected by the people thereof, for six years; and each Senator shall have one vote. The electors in each State shall have the qualifications requisite for electors of the most numerous branch of the State legislatures.

When vacancies happen in the representation of any State in the Senate, the executive authority of such State shall issue writs of election to fill such vacancies: Provided, That the legislature of any State may empower the executive thereof to make temporary appointments until the people fill the vacancies by election as the legislature may direct.

This amendment shall not be so construed as to affect the election or term of any Senator chosen before it becomes valid as part of the Constitution.

Amendment XVIII

Section. 1. After one year from the ratification of this article the manufacture, sale, or transportation of intoxicating liquors within, the importation thereof into, or the exportation thereof from the United States and all territory subject to the jurisdiction thereof for beverage purposes is hereby prohibited.

Section. 2. The Congress and the several States shall have concurrent power to enforce this article by appropriate legislation.

Section. 3. This article shall be inoperative unless it shall have been ratified as an amendment to the Constitution by the legislatures of the several States, as provided in the Constitution, within seven years from the date of the submission hereof to the States by the Congress.

Amendment XIX

The right of citizens of the United States to vote shall not be denied or abridged by the United States or by any State on account of sex.

Congress shall have power to enforce this article by appropriate legislation.

Amendment XX

Section. 1. The terms of the President and Vice President shall end at noon on the 20th day of January, and the terms of Senators and Representatives at noon on the 3d day of January, of the years in which such terms would have ended if this article had not been ratified; and the terms of their successors shall then begin.

Section. 2. The Congress shall assemble at least once in every year, and such meeting shall begin at noon on the 3d day of January, unless they shall by law appoint a different day.

Section. 3. If, at the time fixed for the beginning of the term of the President, the President elect shall have died, the Vice President elect shall become President. If a President shall not have been chosen before the time fixed for the beginning of his term, or if the President elect shall have failed to qualify, then the Vice President elect shall act as President until a President shall have qualified; and the Congress may by law provide for the case wherein neither a President elect nor a Vice President elect shall have qualified, declaring who shall then act as President, or the manner in which one who is to act shall be selected, and such person shall act accordingly until a President or Vice President shall have qualified.

Section. 4. The Congress may by law provide for the case of the death of any of the persons from whom the House of Representatives may choose a President whenever the right of choice shall have devolved upon them, and for the case of the death of any of the persons from whom the Senate may choose a Vice President whenever the right of choice shall have devolved upon them.

Section. 5. Sections 1 and 2 shall take effect on the 15th day of October following the ratification of this article.

Section. 6. This article shall be inoperative unless it shall have been ratified as an amendment to the Constitution by the legislatures of three-fourths of the several States within seven years from the date of its submission.

Amendment XXI

Section. 1. The eighteenth article of amendment to the Constitution of the United States is hereby repealed.

Section. 2. The transportation or importation into any State, Territory, or possession of the United States for delivery or use therein of intoxicating liquors, in violation of the laws thereof, is hereby prohibited.

Section. 3. This article shall be inoperative unless it shall have been ratified as an amendment to the Constitution by conventions in the several States, as provided in the Constitution, within seven years from the date of the submission hereof to the States by the Congress.

Amendment XXII

Section. 1. No person shall be elected to the office of the President more than twice, and no person who has held the office of President, or acted as President, for more than two years of a term to which some other person was elected President shall be elected to the office of the President more than once. But this Article shall not apply to any person holding the office of President when this Article was proposed by the Congress, and shall not prevent any person who may be holding the office of President, or acting as President, during the term within which this Article becomes operative from holding the office of President or acting as President during the remainder of such term.

Section. 2. This article shall be inoperative unless it shall have been ratified as an amendment to the Constitution by the legislatures of three-fourths of the several States within seven years from the date of its submission to the States by the Congress.

Amendment XXIII

Section. 1. The District constituting the seat of Government of the United States shall appoint in such manner as the Congress may direct:

A number of electors of President and Vice President equal to the whole number of Senators and Representatives in Congress to which the District would be entitled if it were a State, but in no event more than the least populous State; they shall be in addition to those appointed by the States, but they shall be considered, for the purposes of the election of President and Vice President, to be electors appointed by a State; and they shall meet in the District and perform such duties as provided by the twelfth article of amendment.

Section. 2. The Congress shall have power to enforce this article by appropriate legislation.

Amendment XXIV

Section. 1. The right of citizens of the United States to vote in any primary or other election for President or Vice President, for electors for President or Vice President, or for Senator or Representative in Congress, shall not be denied or abridged by the United States or any State by reason of failure to pay any poll tax or other tax.

Section. 2. The Congress shall have power to enforce this article by appropriate legislation.

Amendment XXV

Section. 1. In case of the removal of the President from office or of his death or resignation, the Vice President shall become President.

Section. 2. Whenever there is a vacancy in the office of the Vice President, the President shall nominate a Vice President who shall take office upon confirmation by a majority vote of both Houses of Congress.

Section. 3. Whenever the President transmits to the President pro tempore of the Senate and the Speaker of the House of Representatives his written declaration that he is unable to discharge the powers and duties of his office, and until he transmits to them a written declaration to the contrary, such powers and duties shall be discharged by the Vice President as Acting President.

Section. 4. Whenever the Vice President and a majority of either the principal officers of the executive departments or of such other body as Congress may by law provide, transmit to the President pro tempore of the Senate and the Speaker of the House of Representatives their written declaration that the President is unable to discharge the powers and duties of his office, the Vice President shall immediately assume the powers and duties of the office as Acting President.

Thereafter, when the President transmits to the President pro tempore of the Senate and the Speaker of the House of Representatives his written declaration that no inability exists, he shall resume the powers and duties of his office unless the Vice President and a majority of either the principal officers of the executive department or of such other body as Congress may by law provide, transmit within four days to the President pro tempore of the Senate and the Speaker of the House of Representatives their written declaration that the President is unable to discharge the powers and duties of his office. Thereupon Congress shall decide the issue, assembling within forty-eight hours for that purpose if not in session. If the Congress, within twenty-one days after receipt of the latter written declaration, or, if Congress is not in session, within twenty-one days after Congress is required to assemble, determines by two-thirds vote of both Houses that the President is unable to discharge the powers and duties of his office, the Vice President shall continue to discharge the same as Acting President; otherwise, the President shall resume the powers and duties of his office.

Amendment XXVI

Section. 1. The right of citizens of the United States, who are eighteen years of age or older, to vote shall not be denied or abridged by the United States or by any State on account of age.

Section. 2. The Congress shall have power to enforce this article by appropriate legislation.

Amendment XXVII

No law, varying the compensation for the services of the Senators and Representatives, shall take effect, until an election of Representatives shall have intervened.

Additional Sources

In addition to the original text of the US Constitution, the following sources were referenced:

Fiorina, Morris P., Paul E. Peterson, and Betram Johnson. The New American Democracy, Fourth Edition. Pearson Education, Inc., 2005.

Foderaro, Lisa W.. "In Chappaqua, Pride, Dread and a President Down the Street". New York Times September 5, 1999

Killian, Johnny H.. "U.S. Senate: Reference Home > Constitution of the United States". U.S. Senate, S.PUB.103-21, Library of Congress. January 10, 2009 <http://www.senate.gov/civics/constitution_item/constitution.htm>.

Stolberg, Sheryl Gay. "For a Short While Today, It's President Cheney ". New York Times July 21, 2007

Tuleja, Tad. American History in 100 Nutshells. New York: Ballantine Books, 1992.

"CRS Annotated Constitution". Cornell University. 1964-2000 <http://www.law.cornell.edu/anncon/>.

"Distribution of Electoral Votes". Federal Election Commission. October 13, 2003 <http://www.fec.gov/pages/elecvote.htm>.

Made in the USA
San Bernardino, CA
13 August 2017